Pebble® Plus

Cheerleading

Cheers and Chants

by Jen Jones

Consulting Editor: Gail Saunders-Smith, PhD

Consultant: Lindsay Evered-Ceilley
Director of Business Operations
Centerstage Starz Theatre and Dance Studio
Centennial, Colorado

CAPSTONE PRESS
a capstone imprint

Pebble Plus is published by Capstone Press,
151 Good Counsel Drive, P.O. Box 669, Mankato, Minnesota 56002.
www.capstonepub.com

 Books published by Capstone Press are manufactured with paper
containing at least 10 percent post-consumer waste.

Library of Congress Cataloging-in-Publication Data
Jones, Jen.
Cheers and chants / by Jen Jones.
p. cm.—(Pebble plus. Cheerleading)
Includes bibliographical references and index.
Summary: "Simple text and photographs describe cheers and chants and how cheerleaders use
them"—Provided by publisher.
ISBN 978-1-4296-5275-9 (library binding)
1. Cheers—Juvenile literature. 2. Cheerleading—Juvenile literature. I. Title. II. Series.
LB3635.J619 2011
791.6'4—dc22   2010028063

Editorial Credits
Jenny Marks, editor; Ashlee Suker, designer; Wanda Winch, media researcher; Laura Manthe, production specialist;
    Sarah Schuette, photo stylist; Marcy Morin, scheduler

Photo Credits
All photos Capstone Studio/Karon Dubke except: Corbis/Star Ledger/Sarah Rice, 9; Getty Images Inc./Ronald
    Martinez, 11; Shutterstock/Ekaterina Shavaygert, glitter background, Shutterstock/Molodec, star background

Note to Parents and Teachers

The Cheerleading series supports national physical education standards related to forms of
movement. This book describes and illustrates how to use cheers and chants. The images
support early readers in understanding the text. The repetition of words and phrases helps early
readers learn new words. This book also introduces early readers to subject-specific vocabulary
words, which are defined in the Glossary section. Early readers may need assistance to read
some words and to use the Table of Contents, Glossary, Read More, Internet Sites, and Index
sections of the book.

Printed in the United States of America in North Mankato, Minnesota.
092010
005933CGS11

Table of Contents

Author's note: Cheers and chants shown in this book use an **X** to indicate a clap.

X = clap

Winning Messages

Cheerleaders use cheers
and chants to excite the crowd.
Cheers and chants are different.
How do you know which
one to use?

What's the Difference?

Chants are short sayings repeated three or more times. Chants are easy to learn and remember. The crowd can yell along.

Chants are perfect
for exciting parts of a game.
Fans can still watch the action
while cheering.

Shout It Out!

Here we go, Tigers!
Here we go! XX

Chant

X = a clap

Cheers are longer
than chants. They are only
said once. Motions, jumps,
kicks, and stunts make
cheers fun to watch.

Cheers are done during

a pause in the action.

Time-outs, halftime, and

pep rallies are good times

for cheers.

Offense and Defense

Defense chants are about stopping the other team.

Shout It Out!

Go Big D, Hawks!
Hold that line! X

Chant

Offense chants are
all about scoring points.

16

Spirit chants show
team pride.

Shout It Out!

What's your favorite
color, crowd?
Red and black!

Chant

We Love It!

Some cheers tell crowds just what to say. Fans love to be loud and yell along.

Shout It Out!

When we say "go," you say "fight!"
Go! Fight! Go! Fight!
When we say "win," you say "tonight!"
Win! Tonight! Win! Tonight!
Stand up XX
and cheer, XX
for this is our year!

Cheer

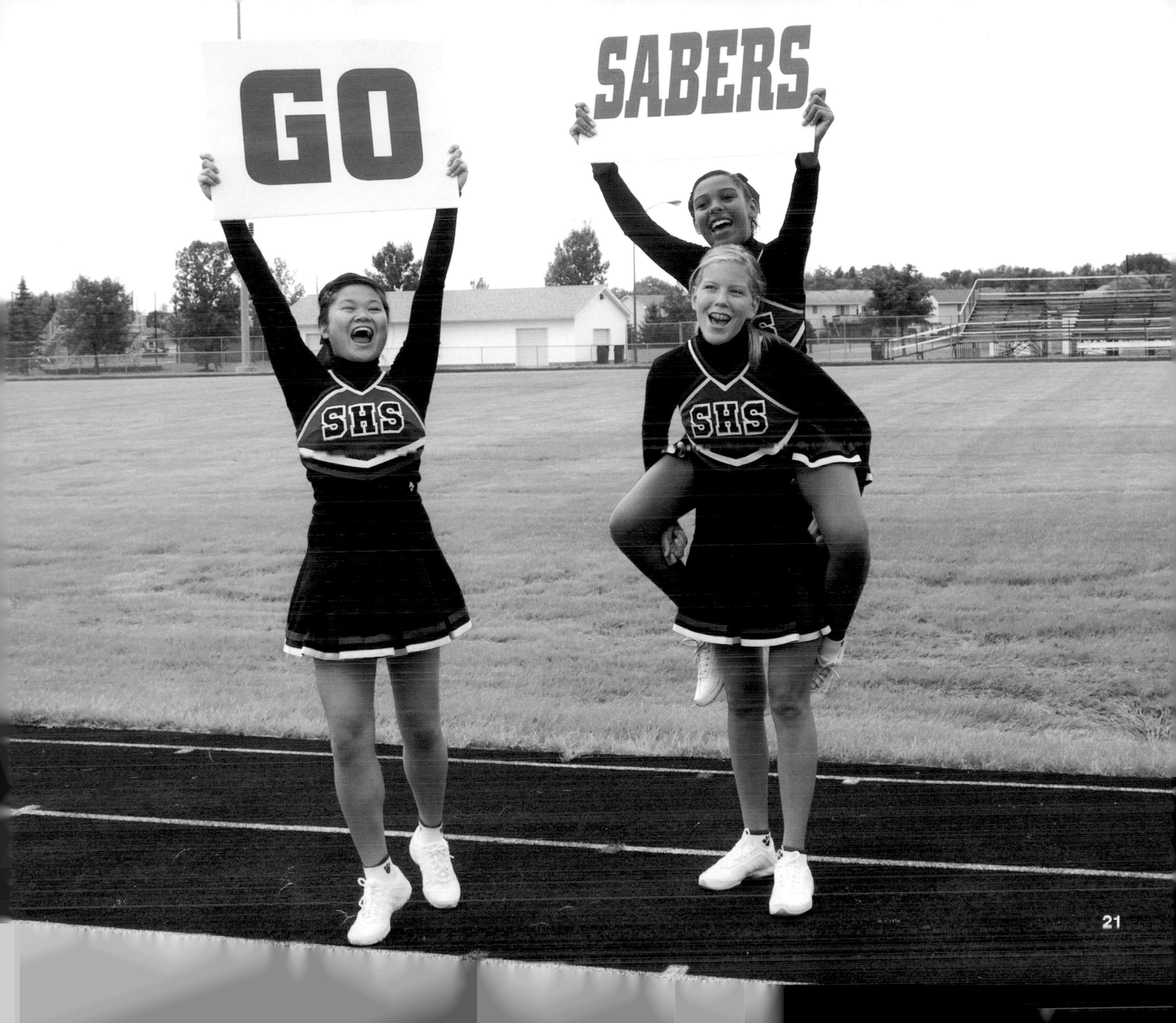
GO
SABERS
SHS
SHS

Glossary

defense—when a team tries to stop points from being scored

halftime—a short break in the middle of a sports game

offense—when a team tries to score points

pride—a feeling of importance or worth

spirit—a feeling of determination and excitement

time-out—a short break during a sports game

Read More

Jones, Christianne C. *Rah-Rah Ruby!* My First Graphic Novel. Mankato, Minn.: Stone Arch Books, 2009.

Karapetkova, Holly. *Cheerleading.* Sports for Sprouts. Vero Beach, Fla.: Rourke Pub., 2010.

Salas, Laura Purdie. *P Is for Pom Pom!: A Cheerleading Alphabet.* Alphabet Fun. Mankato, Minn.: Capstone Press, 2010.

Internet Sites

FactHound offers a safe, fun way to find Internet sites related to this book. All of the sites on FactHound have been researched by our staff.

Here's all you do:

Visit *www.facthound.com*

Type in this code: 9781429652759

Super-cool stuff! Check out projects, games and lots more at **www.capstonekids.com**

Index

Word Count: 134
Grade: 1
Early-Intervention Level: 14